OTHER BOOKS BY JOHN BRADLEY

POETRY
Hotel Montparnasse: Letters to César Vallejo (2021)
Everything in Motion, Everything at Rest (2020)
Spontaneous Mummification (2020)
Agitprop (2019)
Erotica Atomica (2017)
And Thereby Everything (2015)
Love-In-Idleness: The Poetry of Roberto Zingarello (2015)
One Day You a Mountain Shall Be: The Lost Poetry of Cheng Hui (2014)
You Don't Know What You Don't Know (2010)
Terrestrial Music (2006)
Add Musk Here (2002)
To Dance with Uranium (1995)
The New Wine Dreaming in the Vat (1993)
From the Faraway Nearby (1992)
Love-In-Idleness: The Poetry of Roberto Zingarello (1989)
All for Blanca (1988)
A-E-I-O-U (1981)

PROSE
Trancelumination (2011)
War on Words (2006)

ANTHOLOGIES
Eating the Pure Light: Homage to Thomas McGrath (2009)
Learning to Glow: A Nuclear Reader (2000)
Atomic Ghost: Poets Respond to the Nuclear Age (1995)

JOHN BRADLEY

Dear Morpheus, The Glue That Is You

DOS MADRES

2023

DOS MADRES PRESS INC.
P.O. Box 294, Loveland, Ohio 45140
www.dosmadres.com   editor@dosmadres.com

Dos Madres is dedicated to the belief that the small press is essential to the vitality of contemporary literature as a carrier of the new voice, as well as the older, sometimes forgotten voices of the past. And in an ever more virtual world, to the creation of fine books pleasing to the eye and hand.

Dos Madres is named in honor of Vera Murphy and Libbie Hughes, the "Dos Madres" whose contributions have made this press possible.

Dos Madres Press, Inc. is an Ohio Not For Profit Corporation and a 501 (c) (3) qualified public charity. Contributions are tax deductible.

Executive Editor: Robert J. Murphy

Illustration & Book Design: Elizabeth H. Murphy
www.illusionstudios.net

Typeset in Adobe Garamond Pro & Calton Elegance Script
ISBN 978-1-953252-71-5
Library of Congress Control Number: 2022949686

For all those

in need of the balm

of sleep

TABLE OF CONTENTS:

FROM *The Book of Tranquillitatis*

III. *Sleep Furiously Sleep*

From *The Book of Tranquillitatis*

Dear Morpheus,
the Glue That Is You

Colorless green ideas sleep furiously.

–Noam Chomsky

The Book of Tranquillitatis

Be It So: Remember this

Remember this well: calm, cessation, comfort,

dissolve, drift, dormancy, doze, drowse, ease,

hibernate, hush, interlude, lull, oblivion.

Let it overcome each region of the tongue:

pause, quietus, release, repose, rest, settle,

silence, sleep, slumber, somnolence, speechless.

Until there is nothing else but: stay, still, stupor,

suspension, swoon, torpor, trance, tranquil:

tranquility. Until there is nothing else but.

I

Furiously Green Sleep

Dear Morpheus,

Long ago my mother got stardust in her eye; my father
removed it with tweezers.

I was burgled, I was bungled, I was born.
How can I know what to say when you've written my lines

in lime juice and stardust on the bleached sheet?
Let's just admit it—we're all guilty in our every portal

of clandestine stardust-related program activities.
What was it my grandmother said to make me slap her

by accident?
Dust to galactic dust. Milky ash to spiral swirlaway.

However, therefore, nonetheless. Otherwise, finally,
because. Consequently, on the other hand, thus.

Despite everything going on right now, in the interstellar
hush.

Dear Morpheus,

I BREATHE *allegro calmo senza rigore*, which means my legs
rub together calmly yet riotously.
I breathe the Declaration of Interstellar Sleep, though
just hearing this makes me drowsy, which makes me
slightly horny.
I breathe the bird nest baking in the oven, the ovenbird
as it charts unyodeled star formations.
I breathe forge and forger, forgotten and failing to forget, who
sleep undisturbed while sexual dirt asexually breathes.
I breathe tibias napping in a cradle, termites in my tomato soup,
wooden moles mating in a wordless mine field.
I breathe Ishmael, fishmeal, Babylonian email, erotic erratum.
I breathe undigested, undigestible word cloud, drifting
in and out of the visible.
I breathe a bucket of flammable eels, rivers that shed
their skins each moment.

While between each beluga-blue breath, someone near breathes
spontaneous mummification.

I breathe mint, mendicant, meridian, ambidextrous mummy,
the mound digesting a paper clip.
I breathe the desire to fall asleep at 11:11 in a car parked
in the Mississippi.
I breathe chairs made from heron breath, teeth made
from crash dummies, a heart made from a mouthful
of mouth harp.
I breathe oud, cello, kazoo, igloo, hula hoop, hairpiece, ice pick,
macaroni, didgeridoo.
I breathe the sleep that perpetually wakes Sleepy John Estes.

Each breath with no memory of the one just before, no binding
contract for the one to come.
I breathe the unforetold, the untolled passed-back-and-
forth-on-a-levee-one-summer-night breath.
I breathe the roots dangling from *The Disambiguated Book
of Unconfigured Sleep*, my breaths rubbing together riotously
yet calmly.
I breathe unfettered through the many stomachs of you,
dear Morpheus, who has no need of breath, yet allows
these lungs to heave.

WHEREAS:

IF YOU LOVE American history, you love Frederick Douglass

smacking Lincoln with his King James Bible. If you love
Walt Whitman, besotted with his King James Bible,

you love the printing press and the plow, the stiff

white collar and dung-stained dungarees. If you love
Andrew Johnson, playing the marzipan mandolin

at Lincoln's second inaugural, then you love John Brown

swinging his axe deep into his King James Bible,
and all the photographs of the Founding Fathers

in all the American history cookbooks leaking out.

*

One night in the hotel lobby, after the TV
self-detonates, I meet President John Wilkes Booth.

I'm fraught with bluebirds, he says, *frothing bluebirds filling*

the blank spaces all around. Before I strike him on the head
with Clara Barton's King James Bible, I see the holes

in his chest. Clear liquid leaking, dampening the pant legs

of his too-large suit. *Be of good cheer, sir*, I tell President John Wilkes Booth, *for even now blank spaces fill the blank*

spaces all around us with yet more blank spaces.

DEAR MORPHEUS,

DAD BACK HOME in Omaha for the weekend sent me out,
Do I have to?, past the weeping-willow-green-General-Mills-

owned Chevrolet, the one with long eyebrows over
the cat-eyed taillights, out past the radioactive meteorite

in the tall grass field across the street nobody knew who
owned but somebody strung barbwire, past the gypsy

corn stalks, the Otto Graham-signed football rising high
overhead, Sputnik beeped, the President weeped,

Davy Crockett appeared on my pillowcase, and then
slowly faded, we watched dad squander our butter

on his Oreos and then dunk them into his glass
of milk, *He can do it so I can too*, a hog slipping through

Howdy Dowdy's arms in corn-choked Nebraska
on my placemat, the landlady in her phony fur coat

inspecting her property, at night I could hear Hitchcock
fit his portable belly into the belly line, Mom cried

in her sleep, *Starkweather's in the basement with the kids'*
hula hoops, my sister found a centipede in her underpants

drawer, Dad drove us Saturday to *Who made you?*
catechism class, I drew five-pointed stars and played

hangman, a fist struck me in the gut so hard I made
friends with the boiling dust, *You let him do what to you?*

the weeds in the wild field out back on fire, we raked
and raked so the flames couldn't come in, my sister

right behind my rake handle, I gave her for Easter
that year a black eye, Mrs. Parsons when she came

to babysit made us watch Lawrence Welk while she
ate the black bananas, only black bananas, I rolled

down the hill with no brakes and threw myself into
birdwatching and the fat math workbook, all the way

from Omaha to Long Island my brother made us
curse his yellow diaper pail sloshing in the back

of mom's 1953 black Cadillac, with the gas cap
hidden inside the left taillight, I'm not allowed

to talk about Massapequa, but Lynbrook, which
is Brooklyn flipped backwards, that's where we

all sat in front of TV trays, with our Swanson's
fried chicken TV dinners, a bedroom for each

of us in the big white house with a long wooden
ladder to the widow's walk, and with the long

gravel drive I once flew over, none of the kids
noticing me, floating just above them, maybe

it was all that Latin I had to recite at the altar,
where I blacked out at the 6:30 morning mass,

after homework Rodan breaking out of its sleep-
steeped egg for us in that movie over and over

each night for a week on TV, forcing me
to mutter to the basement furnace:

mea culpa, mea—no, non mea maxima culpa.

WHEREAS:

1962: WHAT TO DO when neighbor beats upon neighbor's
Popular Mechanics bomb shelter door. My brother

was about what—four? Ann Henkel—three?

That brick in his hand older and wiser than all
the hurt in the hurt world. Above his head. Over

the wire fence. The brick rose, tottered, falling,

for Mighty Mouse to grab, fell. Mouth open,
Ann Henkel ran inside. Next, her mother

at the fence, forearms pressed to her belly.

Your son, she sang under the pear tree, *dropped a brick
on my daughter's head.* 1962: When he hid inside

the dryer and no one could find him anywhere.

Mom so mad when she pulled him out, she wanted
to drop him off at the convent door, twenty-dollar

bill pinned to his collar. Tell me, brother, what

was it like. So far away from the ache of the turning
world. So still inside that oceanic stillness, still.

WHEREAS:

YOU KNOW this street, you're sure, but
somehow the hushed houses, tilting

trees, bent shadows look unfamiliar.

You find your apartment, approach
the door, a chatty neighbor kid

trailing you. But your key, it doesn't

fit the lock. *Maybe you don't live
here*, says the kid. You try another

door, and this time—relief—the key

slides right in. You notice all the lights
are on, Frank Sinatra's voice purring

in the living room. *Did you leave*

music on? says the annoying kid.
In the bathroom, there's a young

woman in white scrubs. She's tending

three bodies on stretchers. Still
bodies—much too still. *Who*

are you? you demand.

Sanan, she replies. *But I live here*,
you declare, pushing the hardness

of the fact in her placid face.

Not now you don't, she states.
In the basement, you tell your story

to a cop, who nods politely.

When you begin to shout,
he gently places an open hand

on your chest. It feels like a bird,

warm and fragile. *I'll look into it*,
the cop tells you. Which stirs

more anger. Upstairs,

in the bathroom, you hear Sanan
tell one of the patients, *Don't worry.*

This place is now ours.

Dear Morpheus,

LURKING DEEP deep within my throat, each time
I eat, you swallow a bite of me. Spoonful

of clay, forkful of sky. You taste each
word I breach. I chew on the world, word

by marbled word, and you never say:
My dear little bedbug. If not for you,

I would grow ever more infinitely
ethereal. If not for me, you would

grow intolerable in your state of perfect
imperfection. Know I mean you no malice

on winter nights when I linger too long
over my sweet potato and participle soup

and say: *Pretend you do not belong to me.*
Pretend I am not long for you. I will not

tell the Institute of Ethical Dream Control
that you condone Oats with Almonds

& More cereal, that the milk
pooling in the bowl is a galactic portal.

Nor will I confess to those nights
when I hear the ripping of unstitchable

seams and you slip inside
my angelic disorder.

WHEREAS:

MY BROTHER, arms outstretched from his side,
balancing on his nose a large TV, which is

airing an episode of his favorite show–

The Rockford Files. Though the sound
is off and he cannot possibly see

the screen, he provides all the dialogue

perfectly in sync with the actors' lips.
My father, standing on the back of a cow

painted like a zebra, raises an Oreo

over a glass of milk and intones: *Praise ye,*
Lord of sunflower and suicide bomber,

purified poppies and exploding bus,

for all is pleasant and comely in thine eyes.
In the front row, faces painted pancake white,

my mother, sister, and I squirm.

What's wrong with this popcorn? my mother
snaps. *It tastes like burnt kitty poop.*

And why are we the only ones here?

How did I not notice that earlier? I say.
Will you shut the fuck up, my sister replies.

Just watch the damn show before

it's our turn to get out there. Right then
I remember—I left my Swiss army knife

back home in the oven.

WHEREAS:

THE MAN WHO REPAIRED his face with mascara.
The woman who brought her egg cup into the bathroom,

undressed, and bathed before it.

The waiter who patiently waits outside the door
with a fishing knife.

The hand that carries its other hand like a certificate

signed by the paw of a raccoon.
The sound that made listeners drive their cars into

the deepest portion of the river.

My Aunt Betty and Uncle Frank and Cousin Louise
in black licorice shoes melting upon the hot

Brooklyn pavement.

The priest who prays each afternoon by vacuuming
his carpet.

The collar's stiffness around the throat, the throat's

suppleness.
The tow truck driver with the crescent moon scar

at the right corner of his mouth.

The tuning fork found inside the mailbox.
The seal that swims in motions like the sharpening

of a blade, the sweeping of snow.

The charred stick stirring the green pea soup.
The song that made listeners use ballet slippers

for chopsticks.

The tongue, long before you and I and the tongue
ever knew

it was without a brain.

DEAR MORPHEUS,

THE SMELL of creosote. That's when I knew. Know.
You're near. You, once called: Amaziah. Behuel.

Beriah. Shearjashub. Zoheth. You, who listen
to everything I say. Everything I don't.

I'm not sure when I knew. Perhaps in Tuscaloosa.
When I spoke to the cockroach on my bedframe:

Rust in place. And it halted. Turned. Disappeared.
I should have known. That was you

in those words. Long gone. We could all
disappear. At any moment. Except for you.

Wet clover in the rain. Van Gogh telling the fly
on his arm, *You must be kind to all flesh,*

even as you devour it. Was that you, Morpheus?
In his brain stem? Dosing his madness

with broken sleep? Couldn't he smell
the creosote? I try to call out to him now, but

my voice is muffled. As if I swallowed a salamander's
dank breath. A cricket lodged in its throat. All this

can and will appear, disappear. Except for you,
Morpheus. Wet rain on clover.

WHEREAS:

A MOIST, ANONYMOUS brawny brain on a bed,

a soft, red, brainless bed in a room with no features,
no modulation. The brain, without mouth

or visible speakers, addresses you in a pleasing,

unaccented speech: *I appear to be defenseless,
and yet I am not quite what I appear. Shouldn't I*

be disarmed? But haven't I been already?

You stand there, at the foot of the bed, breathing
a bit faster than normal, a cudgel in your hand.

You examine the truncheon, wondering who

gave it to you. On closer inspection, the wooden club
is a book with a thick, slightly damp cover, tiny hairs

waving across the surface. You open the book.

Someone hollowed out the center to hide a handgun
carved out of wood, dyed black with shoe polish.

You stroke the cross-hatched handle. Black

polish stains your finger. Could the gun fire
aimless wooden bullets? You peer down the barrel.

There's something lurking inside. A vine afraid

of the light. The vine gives off a milky scent
that makes you sleepy. When you open your eyes,

all that's left of the handgun is a piece of paper.

You fold and refold it into a bird, fish, a room
with collapsible walls, a piece of wrinkled paper.

Later you come across a clay tile in your back pocket.

Deeply etched lines sketch a slippery brain
shaping itself into a question mark. You turn

the question mark on its side, and it's a handgun

waiting to fire a portion of itself at you. You turn
it back around. No need to be alarmed. No,

it's only a simple pipe evacuating its brain.

Dear Morpheus,

I ASKED the sleep stored in the suitcase
and it said: *I like you too much not to alarm you.*

I asked the motion detector and it said:
Who could harm an ant leaking milk.

I asked the *Book of Trans-Possessive Harmonics*
and it said: *Surrounded by unshaven fire.*

I asked the mole's woven breath
and it said: *Splintered light unfastens its mercy.*

I asked she who stabbed her seat in the cineplex
and she said: *Rain enthralls salted origami.*

I asked the soil swirling in the whirlwind
and it said: *Longing turns the fleeing bee.*

I asked you, dear Morpheus, before you
were Morpheus, before you could not

remember, and you said:
Make your ribs of crave and conjure.

Whereas:

You lie in the road, Marina, unconcerned.
I comb your hair back with my fingers.

I rub nettle on your lips and kiss them.

I rub nettle on your legs, to burn them awake.
Even the rusted garden chair where you used to sit.

Even the wheelbarrow with its rotting wooden wheel.

How can I make your heart beat harder?
Armfuls of tulips tumble through your body.

In your white dress, Marina, that looks like a tablecloth.

I don't care, your eyes say. *I don't care.*

Because hunger cannot eat tulips.
Because hunger can eat tulips and want for more.

You must choose, Marina, the dry leaf, its slow rasp.

The dry garden soil, its purple thistle.
An old man drags through the heat in wool winter coat.

I don't care, your eyes say. *I don't care.*

I rub nettle on your legs and kiss them.
I rub nettle on your lips, to burn them awake.

Be It So: The Nile, as seen

1.

The Nile, as seen from above, weighs 12.80 sidereal ounces. 1,280 tons of cricket parts. 128.0159 billion silted vowels. Laden with insoluble sleep.

2.

That watch at the bottom of the glass of water that gives the exact moment an axe blossoms in the Nile. So that a piano tuner plays underwater. *Feather* and *nether*. An undertaker bee from before the unraveling. That speck of an ant that calls forth a bird that sings of a spore that will be found in your next syllable.

3.

Photo: The Nile as someone's curiously flavorless forearm. Photo: The Nile seeping from holes in your fedora. Photo: The Nile sleeping in your mother's mother's nightgown. Photo: A herd of inflatable poets sipping from the Nile.

4.

What you should know: A voice with no roots pushing out. I place my hand over the hole and hold my breath. Then I hear the voice coming out of a bough just behind. The voice holds on to one word, one sound, and keeps prolonging it, past what's discernible. It's either *moonrobe* or *moonwarble. Moonventricle* or maybe *moonverde*. Oh, I stood under the bough until the voice came out of my foot. My ankle, my leg. I turned around. The voice, as it passed, did not recognize me.

5.

Any fool can find ten hungry flies, she tells me, picking
at her salad. Someone, dear mouth, must be told. That
fleeing substance called *oracular leakage*.

6.

The composer stated, *I was dissecting a crow's throat at the
time. Moontsoaked* or *moonbloat.* The plumber whistled,
tingling the air, which slipped far down the dim drain.
Moonspittle or *moonstippled.* No one remembered to
measure said defendant's right arm. For so many solar
sleeve miles.

7.

The Nile weighs 12.80 pulsations per millisecond. 12.80
tons of cricket halleluiahs. 12.80 humming humming-
bird parsecs. The Nile tickling your aorta as you hear this.
Making sure you breathe in and through. Whatever it is
that sleep cannot

8.

dissolve.

Be It So: I let slide

I let slide a brick. Fitted, one into the other,
unmortared. Slide free the kiln-baked brick—blank.

Not one name. For as you did say: *This is not*

a registry. Where my hand lingers, these markings
appear: *Once again, dear Citizen, record well the faces*

of the few and the many-bruised. Upon your flesh,

inscribe. Upon your fevered forehead, inscribe:
One day an errant scavenger shall assemble from

these very tablets a . . . The lettering lapses

into braided clay, spumed fire. The voice
of a river god when the god was river. *I breathe*

Nile, Euphrates, Ganges, I breathe. Soon the brittle

crumbs crumble. I hold only worn, gnarled teeth
before you. Now, friend Citizen, poured from one

parched palm to another, yours.

BE IT SO: SHOULD I WAKE

1.
Should I wake so I can say, *If only we could sink into
undifferentiated sleep*. Your hair, the sheets, my skin. The
room has drifted closer. In the *Book of Emergencies*, it says,
A wound is a leaf left open. Each time I fall asleep, I wake,
my left hand burning. Instructions on how to bind hair
unto hair calm the air.

2.
Read to me in your sleeping voice how to survive an
emergence.

3.
Where the window used to be, I look. Black string,
orange twine. *Bury it*, you say in your sleep. *Bury it deep to
keep it near.* I smell burning soil. In your hair, the sheets,
my skin. You once said that anyone who uses the words
planetary drift must be sexually hungry. If I can't wake up,
trickle salt into the palm of my hand.

4.
I lean against the doorway watching you (sleep). I swear
I've never seen Stalin's shaving kit. I've never touched his
razor blade rust. Stroked it with my tongue. Infected my
sleep. And yet in an underground train station, I stood
beside a woman with a turtle shell skull.

5.

I hold your silence close. Breathe it in: Stillness in your hair, the sheets, my skin. This could mean I've once seen many small lights flutter around a central light.

6.

To be a mouth around a bee. That need never sleep. Need nothing but furred sleep.

7.

Someone wrote: *Begin the cosmos with a beating crumb.* No one noticed. Instruct me. Instruct the mole on how to be closer to clover drift. Dissolve. This is where the pause swallows the paused. I find it erotic, dear Morpheus, when someone says: *Oh.* The inner mouth hanging open for a second,

8.

letting the outer world spin in.

II

Green Colorless Sleep

Dear Morpheus,

*Have you ever been to Iran
or Iraq?* says the woman

at the registration table.
Knowing the wrong

answer will ban me
from the conference,

I pause. *You know,
I may have accidentally*

*crossed the border once,
lost in eastern Idaho.*

Just a minute, she says,
heading off to consult

someone in a back room.
She comes back with another

question: *Do you ever bear
any scars from the war?*

Which war? I want to ask,
but instead I say, *If peace*

*has taken a bullet
to the head, then*

the heart must think
and pump, pump and think.

She kisses her palm
and then holds it

on top of my head.
I pump and think,

think hard, and then,
harder, pump.

Whereas:

That first time I handled a snake, I was bitten, fell

asleep for three days, and died. My father threw
a bucket of water on me and yelled, *Twenty-five*

push-ups, now. My mother filed her fingernails

and said to my father, *What are you doing, Jack?*
Let him take a little nap. My sister picked up

the long brown snake, let it dangle from her neck,

set it loose in the backyard, near the cesspool.
She came back in and said, *John's not dead.*

He just doesn't want to deliver his newspapers.

That's all. My brother put on my pajamas
and slippers and waved his hands over his head:

I've come back from Heaven! Back from Hell!

Touch my stinky flesh. For only twenty-five cents!
I got out of bed, drank a glass of cold milk,

and delivered all my newspapers. Never said

a word to Vinny, or Micky, or even Leonora
when she wondered about that first time.

WHEREAS:

IT'S NOT EVERY DAY I hear a recording of a photograph
consumed by starlight. My aura, I couldn't seem

to find it today at the corner of Lunch and Divine.

When I came back, there was rice stuck to the bicycle's
handlebars. I found you tangled in the film director's

hairbrush not far from the window. *There's a bird's*

wing stuck under your nose, my wife's left ear signals
to me at the party. The last thing I can remember

is falling asleep in your hand. Every ten seconds

you tell me: *I will let go of you in ten seconds.* I hear them
quarrel at night over the gender of the avocado

in the baby's crib. *Pieces of my hand,* you said looking

at my foot, *were once pieces of a snail.* When my father
jumped out that open door over Sicily, did he call

out *Geronimo?* Or *Morpheus?* Purging me from your

files, you smell of formaldehyde. One word can spin
a lemon into a lime, and two words back into

a wooden egg. Every ten seconds, tell me: *I won't
let go of you for ten seconds.* Someone without

a history of blood needs to record the progeny
of the blade. The moon purring: *Let me sleep,*

my dear, curled in your armpit.

WHEREAS:

THE SMALL SILVER crucifix bearing traces of Drano.

The two-hundred-fifty pound biography of J. Edgar
Hoover, its pages bearing teeth marks.

The parrot who endlessly recites Emily Dickinson's

I'm Nobody! Who the hell are you? to a revolver
at the bottom of its cage.

Julius and Ethel Rosenberg digging their own graves

on the White House lawn.
Frida Kahlo's back massaged with a smooth wooden

spoon by her spider monkey.

The handwritten note in the margin of a collection
of Sappho: *Language is always a modality of desire.*

Specks of lipstick from the lips of Marilyn Monroe

clinging to a toothpick inside an unmarked white-
buffalo-skin envelope.

Julius and Ethel Rosenberg digging up Crazy Horse's

unmarked grave.
A thread of blood zigzagging across the clear glass

dinner plate forming the words: *Paper fan.*

Dear Morpheus,

My FATHER, a bundle of twigs at the side of the road,
bound by rusted twine. Under a sky the color

of once buried silverware, I hoist him on my shoulder.
Q. *But why does the grass fire fear the crow?*

A. *Song doesn't fly from the bird; the sky sticks to the song.*
Snap of twigs breaking as the load jostles.

Q. *Why does the river remember the belly?*
A. *Each day is the dust's birthday.*

Mice-scurry and bird-rustle in the thick twig bundle.
Q. *And why do we smell of unwashed sky?*

A. *Tonight I shall burn to keep your mother warm.*
I shift the load to my other shoulder. I swear. I stumble.

Q. *Why do I stop and toss the bundle to the side of the road?*
A. *Not many will let the moon slip inside the skull.*

Should I sink into the ditch's sleep, or leave
the ditch adrift in sleeplessness?

Q. *Is there no question that will silence you?*
A. *Tonight I shall burn to keep your mother warm.*

Dear Morpheus,

You think I'm carrying an apple, jacked
with sharks' teeth in my backpack. Why don't you

search Joan of Arc's armor? Ask the Attorney
General why he meditates on a photo of Thomas

Merton in his boxers pushing an empty grocery cart
along the beach. If it's true I'm the guy who failed

the postal exam sixteen times, would that make you
more or less likely to hire me as your dirty bomb

detector? My father's jacket at the rummage sale,
the pocket holding a line from *Autobiography of a Guar*

Gum Salesman, now illegible. If you've peed into
the *I Heart NY* coffee mug, then you can't avoid

crossing a golf course without lightning firing
your dura mater. I carry a small drill bit dangling

from my neck so if I ever get locked in a trunk
I can engrave my obituary into the shell

of a bituminous turtle. Every night in your cellar
the actor who plays Eurydice swallows another

gnawed-upon olive pit and then the war goes on.
The eyes sting a little at first, and then—everything

shine-shine-shines like the seat
of my schoolboy gabardines.

Dear Morpheus,

A SMALL PIECE of sky, unquiet
blue. I hold it in my palm

and let it shimmer. But
what was it I came here to say?

Perhaps:
Though a small part

of the vast machinery of sleep,
I, too, breathe delirium blue.

WHEREAS:

1.
MAYBE I LEFT IT in the men's room, the way I sometimes
forget my ring on the ledge above the sink

after washing my hands.

How am I going to be able to relieve myself now?
Shoulder me.

2.
At least I have my tongue.

3.
I know it was there when I was in the car. I could feel
the bulge in my pants as I watched the long legs

of the yellow jacket delicately stroke the red pine needle

on the windshield. Maybe it fell out of my pants
when I stepped out of the car.

Shoulder me. At least I still have my teeth.

4.
What would anyone want with a penis, with *my* penis,
anyway? A woman once told me she dreamed

she was carrying my penis around with her all day long

in her handbag. Was this a compliment? A complaint?
After the slaughter at Sand Creek, soldiers rode off

with the sexual skin of Native American women

on their hats. Shoulder me.
It's a good thing I still have my liver.

5.
If I wear the Hawaiian shirt with the red and orange

pineapples, no one will notice the void in my pants.
Maybe. No matter what, though, shoulder me,

I still have my, shoulder me, not-yet-missing tongue.

Dear Morpheus,

A RAZOR BLADE glides along, shines
alongside. All the spirits want

the green lurking within the red
tongue. The sound of an ant wandering

within an earlobe. The farmer
suspending his belly above the history

of want. John Lee Hooker stirring
his whiskey milk with a missing

wooden finger. O to be done with
the undone. The neighbor's rat

chewing a hole in the Thursday sky
at the edge of the river. Stir the dust

with a twig to make it wiser
than wind. I placed only a trace

of winter on your grave. *Love one
shoe, lose the other*, goes the insomnia-

infested song. I never saw you wrestle
the three-legged spirit to the ground

but I saw the ground surround you. Watch
me glide along, fly alongside,

still breathing 1939.
O to be done.

Dear Morpheus,

Break open any one of us, and you'll find,

should you ever unremember, what
you dislike about us. Should you recall that

error, you'll find baked clay teeth, glazed hands

ready to grip any glowing ember, ready
to embrace a half-baked shoulder. Should you

ever disremember what so disturbs us,

our underbaked brain, fire-crazed hands, each
gripping a sickle piece of the moon, to wave

before each other. If you ever remember this

earth, this kiln, where you appear amongst us,
much too much, we fear, like us. Though we

fire each wobbling word through the woven

sky. Though we know you never read, dear
Morpheus, what's composed with lingual fire.

Dear Morpheus,
This Too Is Topographically True

1. Draw my face out of your tibia, my hands with chuff and charcoal.

2. Draw rectangular black bands over the eyes of my father, an Irish bog swaddling my mother.

3. Draw me looking confused and calm, holding a placid bomb, a frightful balm.

4. Draw to your side *Silence: An Abbreviated Interruption.*

5. Draw a wasp navigating the sky inside a big-mouthed glass jar. Don't be alarmed if I ask you for your zip code and a recent soil sample.

6. Draw me in your lower bowel, my thumb a toad that resembles a leaf, a leaf that resembles a war that resembles red dust.

7. Draw a wristwatch placed on a tree stump next to an unidentifiable blue-black turd. Photograph the drawing, then fax the drawing of the photo.

8. Draw, over a foliated field, a cheesecloth sky. Trace the exfoliated lines that leave no trace.

9. Draw the sewer system with an olive pit and the red-tailed hawk with the cries too shrill to draw.

10. Draw a tomato with tangerine urges. *Be wary of molten pulp*, says the wasp, full of unenumerated silence.

11. Do not attempt to draw this: Swallow a pair of dull scissors. Lie down on spent newsprint. Without moving, cut an entry for a drawn-out exit.

12. Draw me yawning, drawing your face floating over Iceland, nearly dawn.

Dear Morpheus,

I learned to abide—if I may steal your
term—with the help of envelopes.

I would surrender a fallen hair. Split
fingernail. Into an envelope. Write

the date, time, weather, location. Seal it
with tallow and lynx breath. Arrowroot

and pepper spray. A shard of Lincoln's
Mt. Rushmore eyebrow. The running fear

that can be stolen from a sleeping vole.
The winter of a muskrat lodged

in the back of your leg. The lovely
tastelessness of lunar dirt. Everything

that grows grows calm after the turtle shed
its shell. Over his corpse, we buried the door

to his tool shed. To her bedroom door.
Make my mask with the back of the leather

coat he wore. Pineal gland. Rib. Soon you
too shall chew upon the cornice of the moon.

WHEREAS:

1. THROUGH THE GRAVEL parking lot, I dragged my suitcase, tottering on its too small wheels.

2. If you can pack a banana inside a lemon inside a cranberry.

3. It might be useful to know I once borrowed two black leather boots from the entryway of Tom McGrath's house. My shoes soaked. Socks soaked. I swear I meant to leave a Writ of Seizure on the door.

4. Then George pulled the earbud from his left ear, and said, *Why are you dragging a vacuum cleaner behind you?*

5. I had a fist class ticket to Addis Ababa, a roundtrip ticket to Kuala Lumpur, a one-way ticket to Grand Forks. Though I had been given no instructions whatsoever on how to remove the paring knife lodged between my radius and ulna.

6. Pack a plum into a prickly pear into an avocado.

7. In the large open room, I could hear a man in a blue jean jacket chatting with a woman in the kitchen making coffee.

> *Be not afraid to swallow, to scrub*
> *your insides with coffee containing*
> *seven, fourteen, maybe twenty-two*
> *grains of sand.*

8. Be not afraid of Tom McGrath, please.

9. A Medusa-headed mop, a windshield wiper, a cracked blackboard, an open box of Cheerios, a lamp with a black glove over the bulb.

10. I'm sure George was listening to Georges Desnos giving a recitation of *A Brief Guide to the Anti-Universe* scrawled on the inner-heart of a mole rat.

11. She said she kept a wild horse in the closet, a quiet, unobtrusive horse that ate dry cereal and would speak at times when not spoken to.

12. I could hear McGrath say, *What did you do to disrupt the war?*

13. A persimmon disguised as a pomegranate hidden in a guacamole piano.

14. Wandering down the corridor with a dark granite floor, I could hear the horse's delicate voice, all too near.

> *I could hear, underneath the flooring, strands of barbed wire twisting, stretching. Twenty-two strands. Sprouting hair. No, not hair, but velour, soft and fine.*

15. There's only so much you can say to someone across a large open room. Only so much that will fit into the hold of a shout.

16. Not that I was anywhere in the vicinity of the horse that could allegedly emit speech. But I could hear it quietly confide: *Patriotism is the poison we feed to the gods.*

17. For some reason, my fingers fumbled with the buttons of my shirt.

18. I looked behind me, and yes, I was pulling a vacuum cleaner, tottering on its too small wheels.

19. In the parking lot, I saw a soldier in a silver-blue sedan, and I waved, thinking this must be my ride. He stared, as if there were a photo of the burned face beneath my face.

20. The soon-gone, the already-left, the still-going-who didn't-yet-know-they-disappeared-long-ago. I could taste them, at eighteen, in the back of my mouth.

21. Tell them, tell everyone, what I did during the war. I buried, behind the garage, Amelia Earhart's goat-horn saxophone.

22. Whenever I could. Whenever I can.

Dear Morpheus,

I KNOW WHY you say, *I shall abide
with you*. To cool all flesh that throbs

and itches. How we've clawed
at scabs that refused to be salved.

How we've lurched and scratched
in bouts of unstitched sleep.

Because you shall dwell one day
within us, no back or chest or brain

will itch or swell another night.
A smooth, soothed itchlessness

shall engulf us. Our glassy flesh
the temperature of fire-laced ice.

Because you, Morpheus, shall slay
each breach of unsutured sleep.

Or so you say.

BE IT SO: IN THE BABBLE

1.

In the babble behind each blur, you can hear dear Morpheus.
If only I could claim, *My father invented the ant that
eats aluminum.* That photo of James Dean in fetal sleep
at the back of the bus makes me want to say, *Let's hear
your seventy-seven volume* Ode to Styrofoam. I feed my
buttonholes sawdust, something I've never told anyone,
not even my lawyer's goldfish. Or is it a piranha?

2.

But I've never knowingly harmed the polar moon, I repeated
to the judge, who that day was a Bo Diddley hologram,
who decreed, *When we wake music, who knows what we
wake. Serve only the silence that lies open to every unguent.*
In the wooden ambulance, I lie on my side, on leaves left
by passersby.

3.

My scar, she told me, *wakes me up at night asking for an
invocation for earthquake, earache, avalanche.*

4.

When ready, place your tongue in the river's seam, you tell
me, *thus altering the course of the narrative.* All this makes
me boundless uncomfortable, right where my stomach
was last located, next to the eel skin sofa. The antidote
for boredom will be a toxin for which no antidote has yet
been invented. That photo of you weeping in Rome after
reading *Ode to Styrofoam.* She insisted she hadn't dined on
a dead bicycle in years.

5.
Please don't make that cranial croak if I say I choose
to never sleep with you in a silver soup ladle again.
Someone should record this on an eyelash with a laser.
An invocation to ward off panacea and logorrhea. In the
wooden ambulance, I lie on my side, on a cloud of vowels
left by passersby.

6.
Ah, Morpheus, if you only knew what the moon does
each night with your black latex glove.

Be It So: A small-winged

1.

A small-winged thing flutters overhead.

2.

I'd shoved against the heavy door to enter. In the dense dark, I waited for my eyes to tell me what I could see. I crept to a pew in the front to sit beside a woman with a moon face. Then, on my right, a man with enormous hands clutching his crumpled hat squeezed in. I slid over ever closer to the woman, my thigh pressing against her warm thigh. She turned, glared at me. I stood up, slipped past the man with the mishappen hat, wandered off.

3.

In the dimness that settled in the far back of the church, I could smell incense seeping out of the rotten wood planks of a porch that could have once been an altar. I could taste the silence—once a surging music—ground down into a red metallic dust.

4.

A small-winged thing flutters overhead. Lilac-colored fuzz, small gold beads, and dried moss adorn it. At the end of the pew, the man with enormous hands reaches out toward the fuzzy flying thing. Now the creature hovers before my face. I let my hand surround it, gently. Then open. Let it go.

5.

Look. There's a welt, where the delicate fuzz brushed my flesh. Injecting some kind of venom. Now my left hand looks mottled. Yellow and black, my thumb throbs. *Let your beloved poison depart you*, the moon-faced woman tells me. *Let it go.*

6.
A small-winged thing flutters overhead. I lift up my hand, now glass, lilac-colored glass.

Be It So: From room to room

1.

From room to room I go with an empty glass of sleep in
my hand. I go from stairway to laundry room but the
door, it interposes a stop made of steel. I could forgive
the cat's vomit on the rug, the undigested pellets soft
but clinging still to recognizable form. I forgive you,
Morpheus, because I forgive the cat her kidneys shutting
down, though I cannot excuse her kidneys for doing what
they do, in the basement, to the cat. The door gives a
little, but not enough. Some force, some farce, behind the
door won't let me carry on as I have before.

2.

I can feel velocity slaying the heart.

3.

If I had a tuning fork, I could hear Generalissimo
Francisco Franco interrogating his bowels, singing off key,
to ease his constant constipation. Franco's buttery words
flutter off, and he chases after them, lurching into the
cosmos a lullaby only Miguel Hernandez could carve out
of calcified turd. I could hear Josefina nibbling at the end
of her hair, her husband's final year. Manuelito recording,
with paint brush dipped in breast milk, *How to Swallow
the Moon in Twenty-Six Simple Steps.*

4.

This is no time to douse your shoes with sawdust and
starfish powder.

5.

The door pushes back, the steel bolt ready to lock me into
my glasses, my glass of water, the cat's broken kidneys,
my growl so much like a grovel. If I forgive you, steel
door, then I must forgive the audience who cringes at the
proper moment to fling change on stage. The custodian,
asleep in my seat, who cleaned his nails with a silver
toothpick. Still, the steel door gives a bit when against it I
heave my vaporous weight.

III

Sleep, Furiously Sleep

Dear Morpheus,

You lose your way each time I tell you
you pour your face into my hands.

Someone wrote these exact words
using candles nothing like these.

I pull a choir out of my femur, hang it
from a tree until it dissolves.

As a vowel travels from your diaphragm
into the throat of your nipple,

I let in someone who looks something
like you, who seems almost leaden.

Pull a pitcher out of my spine and then
pour the night back into the spinal book.

Endless is my vow. Every day
contains the hiss of history.

I always almost forget: Your face
is not the same as what comes after this.

Dear Morpheus,

That shirt I buried belonged to my father, his life-
span of breathing dirt. I didn't care that the shirt

would remain alive and alert in the dirt. Oh, to dig
a shirt out of the earth and wear it for a little

while above the dirt. It wasn't that the shirt had
had relations with some malodorous dirt. I should

let the dirt bury whatever it wants to bury
in the dirt. *Dirt to dirt*, I said over the hole

in the earth, *shirt to shirt*. As we all know, a shirt
should never be worn by shapeless or even shapely

dirt. I should never have listened to those holes
eating the collar of the shirt. I buried the shirt

because . . . because all around me there was so much
dirt. I should not have let something that commingled

with skin commingle with dirt. I don't really want
to know what happens when dirt begins to inhabit

a shirt. I've buried the ashes of a sickly cat,
a contaminated book, but never a still-breathing shirt.

If only I'd listened to the sky and let the shirt expire
in a tree like withered dirt. And if the shirt should

rise up and flail its flimsy arms, flinging loose
pebbles and dirt? Oh, to fall through to earth

and vanish at the same moment as your earthly
hurt. Before my first, after the last, articulated dirt shirt.

Dear Morpheus,

I was gathering electricity with a spoon. You were living
in Hong Kong with that guy who liked to say: *No one*

*wants to fall in love with a shoe worn by someone who had cancer
of the tongue.* I never met a matchstick that didn't say:

Oh, don't worry. I know when to stop. On the Washington
Avenue Bridge, he was selling vials of Bob Dylan's rain-

water. *To help speed the end of all desire*, he said. We have
in common that vein that throbs ecstatically. *One day*

a month, you promised, *I'll let my mouth go fallow.* That
musky fish bowl on top of your TV. Instead of a ring,

you wore a Ben Franklin rolled around your wedding
finger. Place another mountain inside my backpack.

Please don't tell me again that I never met a spud
I didn't like. More than weather resides in that hole

in the side of the catalpa. Everything appears more
apparent when that mustard stain on my shirt mutters:

I know when to stop. She cursed me in Latin and I thought
it was a blessing. That musky fishbowl on your rusted

TV. To be injected with a small dose of the Sea
of Tranquility to make you immune to the moon. Right

after he said nothing, he said, *I don't want to be erased.*
To ease the world's end. Is, was, why.

Dear Morpheus,

I'm not feeling so well in my ethereal
regions. Translation: Someone misspelled

misspelled, enraging the fury of the dura mater
fires. I can tell you this: the tick's blood

song will long outlast the tick. Translation:
Water is flesh, whether from the river

or fallen from the beak of a wren.
I went out the front door, got lost

on the third step, tried to come back inside,
and the door wasn't living where it last resided.

Translation: Never argue with anyone
with an eel swimming inside the bladder.

Translation: Blockage could take the form
of a neighbor, radio host, muskrat hair.

Translation: Making a mark in the river
with your collarbone, that's one way. Now

I've exited my head through the fontanel, so
far away I can feel myself drifting back

into the dura mater, seeping through.

WHEREAS:

IT'S TRUE, my brother once carried a police badge,
maybe to arrest the gnawing at his bones. Maybe

for the thrill of yelling—*Police! Freeze!* Watching

some John's eyes and nostrils widen. The heart
thrashing against its battered cage. My brother

used to trap muskrats and sell their fur. Whenever

I see a muskrat now in the Kishwaukee, I pretend
I've freed it from my brother's trap. If he read this,

my brother would laugh, call me a *wussy*. Once,

he carried a police badge until that day he pulled it
on a real cop. Eyes, nostrils widening. The heart

thrashing against its flimsy cage. The last time

we spoke—before he begged a knotted sheet to still
the gnawing—that night he told me: *Mom will outlive*

us all. He laughed. I laughed. The ever-expanding

cosmos, it kept expanding. Sometimes, for just
a quiet moment, within its unquiet cage, the heart

quells. Let it. I say, let it try to arrest this world.

WHEREAS:

HOLDING THE SCULPTURE of the head

in his hands, Jack Spicer could be kissing
himself, the craters of Mars, or the state

of California. Why not? This could be

the head of Orpheus at three in the morning
just after Eurydice's hand stroked his face

too softly. Before she turned back down

the aisle stocked with pet food, bird cages,
and salt blocks. Then she dissolved in that space

near the rest rooms where the sleepless linger,

not knowing just what they're looking for.
Orpheus's face stinging with Eurydice's last

words: *What have you done, you dear, darling fool?*

Spicer knows he's kissing someone who died
with a poem on the tongue, a poem that could

poison any feathered creature that flits from throat

to branch to sky. Jack knows this plaster head
can never speak. Lie. Anesthetize. Never sing.

But oh, those cold, luscious lips.

Dear Morpheus,

Yes, I once slightly injured Henry David Thoreau
when I slammed the car door on his thumb

after he corrected how I said his last name.
My sister keeps a loaded Colt .45 duct-taped

to the bottom of her desk. When the security
guard told me to remove my fingerprints, I noticed

in the floor an embedded onion. On the form,
where it asked for my profession I inscribed,

in tiny print, "When I Heard the Learn'd Astronomer."
Whenever I hear the word *infinitesimal,* my spleen

wants to sob. At the post office, the reclusive
opera star wears gold slippers and a hummingbird-

feather coat so no one would recognize him.
Tell them I don't do nude scenes, and I won't peel potatoes

under a new moon, said my mother. I confess I was
the one who plugged my finger into the hole

in the side of the *Titanic* and then threw up
during the credits, where for every role

your thumbprint, Morpheus, appeared.

WHEREAS:

I WROTE A LETTER to the moon with breast milk and arsenic.

I wrote a letter to the teeth of Paul Celan with an icicle
dipped in solar salt.

I wrote a letter to Joan Baez, asking her if we were married

during the year I was living inside a wandering mailbox.
I wrote a letter to the KKK asking them if it was true

that they were the Kalamazoo Kosmic Klezmer band.

I wrote a letter to Dorothea Lange's camera, describing
the diagram Euclid drew of a tongue intersecting a wet plum.

I wrote a letter to Laika, the Soviet space dog, but it was

delivered to a tiny snail shell.
I wrote a letter to the moon using a crow feather dipped

in the Gobi.

I wrote a letter to the Tower of Babel, but it was delivered
to a stolen white tuba.

I wrote a letter to a murmuring mound that moves

from place to place one grain at a time.
I wrote a letter to Machu Picchu, using only the words

further and *flutter* and *farther*.

I wrote a letter to Thomas Merton, each word tied
by a thread to the breeze stirred by a bee's wing.

I wrote a letter to Covid-19, but it had to be burned

thirty-nine times, the ash cauterized.
I wrote a letter to the Eiffel Tower, but it was delivered

to a warehouse of untranslatable faces.

I wrote a letter to the pomegranate on the kitchen
counter, too gnarled and brown to be broken open

to eat those juicy, red carpet tacks.

I wrote a letter to my father falling from the night
sky; he's trying to read the Gospel of the Ant-Lit Asteroid

by flashlight as he's falling, sand leaking from his

left boot.
I wrote a letter to my baby teeth, but when I placed

my ear to the envelope, I heard someone tossing dice

into a hot frying pan.
I wrote a letter to the day I was born, which wrote

a letter to the day the alphabet will be devoured

by a poisoned armadillo.
I wrote a letter to Fulang Chang, Frida Kahlo's naughty

pet monkey; the letter smelled of a fish in the pocket

of an asbestos raincoat.
I wrote a letter to Herbert Hoover, or was it J. Edgar

Hoover, asking how to boil the weevils out of the *Book*

of Infested Insomnia.
I wrote a letter to Elizabeth Bishop's toucan, Uncle

Sam, using smoke from Krakatoa.

I wrote a letter to Lorine Niedecker, cutting small squares
and triangles from a leaf throbbing with liquid light.

I wrote a letter to infinity, which wrote a letter

on the back of my head, saying: *Tell me long and slow*
in Sumerian everything we owe.

Dear Morpheus,

Though it's already morning, I need somewhere to lie
this heavy body down. There's a wooden sign

on the nearby yellow house that reads: *SLEEP
FOR RENT*. I knock on the door and a sullen woman

appears. I tell her of my need. She pauses, pushes
the door open wider, turns, and I follow. She leads me

to her garage, the open side door. *You'll have to pay*,
she says, as if testing me, *for last night*. I'm so tired

I agree. She points to the beds with her chin
and murmurs, *You can have the one with the crib railing*.

I look around. What she calls a bed is a blanket, folded
lengthwise in half, spread out on the concrete floor,

with a pillow. There are two rows of these so-called
beds, three feet apart. Unsure of which bed she means,

I wander amongst them. A few renters stroll off
into the morning glare, having had their fill of sleep.

I want a bed away from the door, away from the light,
but I notice something has been scattered over several

of the blankets—dried brown pellets. They look like
cat food, though I see no cat about. I end up back near

the door and find the bed I've avoided has no brown
pellets strewn across the blanket. Then I see a wooden

railing, broken from playpen or crib, leaning against
the garage wall. This must be the bed the landlady

told me to take. I lie down on the blanket, the concrete
floor pressing hard, the sun boiling in the window,

burning through my eyelids, through my jellied eyes,
to the brain's pulsing core. There's nothing to do

but lie still and mutter: *Morpheus, come find me,*
hold me in your long, bony arms.

WHEREAS:

I MUST FEED the moon, you say, as you turn
the wheel, grinding gelid night stars into ever

bright pablum. It's wrong, though, to consume

living light. *Nothing can be more right than riven salt,*
when silted with kindness, you tell the stars, as you

grind their shine into swirling powder on the small

ceramic plate. But you are captive here, Star-Grinder,
bound by celestial task, punished for bringing edible

light into this inevitable world. *Stand back*, you warn.

Few can resist the shifting, sifted light. But why,
my lower back asks, why cage the curling crescent

moon? Soundless as moth crumb. Why forever

feed on its unending hunger? *I must follow this*
spoon, you note, *into the merest mouth. Even*

as it glows with the shine of skull. But why? Why not

let the moon glaze our flesh? Let it feast on vowel
of owl and vole. Silence. *I must feed the moon,*

you say, grinding the cosmos into dust.

WHEREAS:

AFTER WE'RE GONE, alien historians will say

how we fashioned, each day, a wormwood
chalice.

    Only to break, each night,

the delicate stem. Only to drink in
the bitter galactic vapor within.

       Again.

Dear Morpheus,

I BREATHE Ten Sleep, Wyoming; Sleeping Bear Dunes,
Michigan; Sleepy Eye, Minnesota.
I breathe Zoheth, Shearjashub, Beriah, Behuel.
Amaziah, I breathe.
I breathe *allegro calmo senza rigore*, which means my legs
rub together calmly yet riotously.
I breathe the ladder in my bed that breathes my inner ear.
I breathe at the corner of Curb and Delay, Lunch and
Divine, Mercy and Retrieve, in the Year of Boiled Sleep.
I breathe the dirt in my dirt shirt as it expands and expires,
returns, respires.

I breathe, whenever possible, that infinitesimal infinity
you ask for, whenever I breathe.
I breathe pulverized sleep cleaved back together
at 9:41:41.
I breathe a baby with a gun humming its gums
on an elevator with a lawyer in my spine.
I breathe lubricant zone, ethereal nostril, wall sealant,
breathing eyelid of a dreaming ant.
I breathe someone with a Milky Way accent, which means
I linger too long in your left lung.
I breathe paring knife and collarbone long after you've gone
to devour another breath.
I breathe Buster Keaton's breathless romance with Emily
Dickinson, her suitcase full of day lilies.

Breathe, breath. Breath, breathe. Out of respect
for infinity. Out of respect for spontaneous
mummification. Beluga-blue breath.

I breathe the hiss of history long after the spoken reaches
the sodden and the sudden.
I breathe the roots dangling from *The Disambiguated Book
of Unconfigured Sleep*, my breaths
rubbing together riotously yet calmly.
O to breathe the breath of a mineralogist, elbow to elbow.
Is and will and never was.
I breathe I breath I breathe underwater origami a bit
lighter each time I breathe.
I breathe unfettered through the many stomachs of you,
dear Morpheus, who has no need
of breath, yet allows these lungs to heave.

Dear Morpheus,

SPEAK to my gut, a glass of sand, pinprick of blood.
The more I babel my tongue, the more I bite it. Each

time one less lunar concerto, one more listing crow.
Dissolve my internal warts. Sleeping with a map

underneath the mattress pulls a tart apple in five
directions. Only at the aviary could I find a breadcrumb

in the shape of a bird with a feathered tongue. In Omaha,
I began to draw on my body all the swifts one river

can bear. Talk to my tongue, glass of sand, pinprick
of ink. Dissolve my internal wants. Expel that sing-song

voice: *Shall I inflate the crows now? I won't inflate them
in the house this time, I promise.* Draw to me

all the feathers one body can bear. Let them stick
everywhere. Dear Morpheus, the glue that is you.

FROM:

The Book of Tranquillitatis

Be It So: You shadow me

I.
You shadow me far enough behind to be my brother,
but never close enough so I can ask. Did you ever finish
that book about Houdini in the next life writing on the
bathroom mirror with a bar of soap a message to his
wife in the bathtub, hand dangling over the side? All
these purple paper clips in my pocket—I have to get
them back in dad's desk drawer before I can sleep. I draw
maps of tongues, all sizes and shapes, the intersection of
pronunciation and future income. Your brown brogans,
two sizes too big, you stuff with newspaper in the toes,
which makes them go *squish, squish.* When I open dad's
desk, there's that small drawer I can't find the key to that
you once told me you opened with a black Lab's incisor.

2.
I draw maps of dragonflies trapped inside a donkey's
bladder.

3.
Something's humming in here. Can you hear it? I say to
my mother, who slips into the room just as I sidle away
from the desk. I once won a medal, busy with bronze
bumps, which I lost long ago, for drawing a map while
blindfolded of a mountain range that melted into black
licorice. If you look up at the sky and a raindrop—
traveling at speeds only a liquid crow can know—passes
through your pupil, it will take eons before it arrives at
the point of departure. A car pulls off the road and comes
to a skidding stop, the driver scribbling on his hand a

word made of circles and squares. If I get out the frying pan and start scrambling some eggs, sprinkling on top some chopped black olives and feta, please, sit at the table with me for a bit.

4.

Pretend you want to stay. You want to say: *To linger in the lilt of the tongue.* When I get out of bed, I know what I'll find in my pocket—a map of long fingers stuffed with cow nipples and red silk. Downstairs someone's going *squish, squish.*

5.

You know I'll do most anything in defense of the sleepless tongue.

Be It So: There is only one

1. There is only one nightingale, dear Petitioner of Sleep, and it tastes of winter night and galled glue.

2. Observe the wrist. Observe the nightingale's distant drift across your brow.

3. If I possessed both calm and chaos, I would break the peacock into a thousand thousand threaded starlit gills.

4. Just because your wear a sandy tidal gown over your solids and stripes doesn't mean that history isn't gathering at your groin.

5. I once rented wing and space, but I had to pawn them for a cup of soil.

6. Let me palpitate in your palm; then the moon won't be seen bleeding light through our eyes.

7. John Keats worked as a gandydancer whereupon he built a mechanical songbird for his beloved. She bathed; the nightingale song dissolving into her flesh; her mind took flight. Now she recites without rest, without mercy, enthralled.

8. *That's an awful lot of words*, she said, toting a bucket brimming with liquid vowel.

9. Let the table, let the breadcrumbs: Tumble back into cricket and ink.

10. I feed Morpheus this hominid house, and Morpheus lets fall a febrile larynx into the bush that's sometimes a mailbox and sometimes a crow.

11. After the last word expires, we shall close every opening and let drift take us back to the place where every sound unspools.

12. Those aren't nightingales—they're knots where the night finds itself bound to the edge of your brow.

13. Night above and below. I must go forth and make the song a buried ear can hear. These endnotes on a location some call *Dear Morpheus, Even As Our Flesh Is Infiltrated by Ethereal Unguents from Afar.*

14. To fill the pulsating holes, starless and bottomless, with pulverized sleep.

Be It So: Comfort us

Comfort us with lavender, chamomile, goat bladder.
With magnolia bark, valerian root, powdered shark tooth.
Comfort, with cello and bassoon, this unquiet flesh.

: flesh observed by the Bureau of Nongeometrical Sleep
: flavored with slices of boiled silence
: flesh as seen from just above and just below the aorta
: viewed through a hole in a ragged star

Comfort us with oceanic trumpet and cranial ocarina.
With bits of lightning and chewed aluminum.
Comfort us unto the root of the root of our flesh.

: flesh asleep on a damp sheet of microbial music
: massaged with a heated ceramic hand
: flesh made from bread, bream, retinal stream
: smelling of coffee, radar, starling lament

Comfort the purged, the paused, the surged.
The wandering mass grave with its steep, rock-embedded feet.
Comfort deep the nettle and the flesh.

: flesh listening to the sulking egg timer
: flesh from an archangel with antifreeze for blood
: each pore murmuring: *alveolar moon*
: flesh soothed by interstellar tongue drift

Comfort us with convulsive bolts of black silk.
Comfort us where we can't, and won't, and nonetheless.
Collide us. Fracture. Collapse us into sleep.

NOTES:

Page xi, "Colorless green ideas sleep furiously" is a sentence composed by Noam Chomsky in 1957, intended to show how grammar can be correct and yet create "nonsense." Perhaps Chomsky inadvertently reveals how "nonsense" and poetry can at times feel like kin.

Page 4, "Whereas: If you love": Clara Barton, John Wilkes Booth, Frederick Douglass, Andrew Johnson, and Walt Whitman all attended Abraham Lincoln's Second Inaugural.

Page 8, "*mea culpa, mea—no, non mea maxima culpa.*" In the Latin mass, the litany is "*Mea culpa, mea culpa, mea maxima culpa*": "through my fault, through my fault, through my most grievous fault."

Page, 49, "Whereas: Through the gravel" is in memory of Tom McGrath.

Page 69, "Whereas: Holding the sculpture" is for George Kalamaras, who composed the first line of this poem, which was inspired by Robert Berg's photo of Jack Spicer kissing a bust of the head of Jack Spicer.

Page 76, "Whereas: *I must feed*": Inspired by Remedios Vara's painting *Celestial Pablum*.

Page 83, "Be It So: You shadow me" is in memory of my brother, Dan.

ACKNOWLEDGMENTS:

With deep gratitude to these friends for their guidance and support: Bonnie and Ric Amesquita, Marilyn and Cliff Cleland, Joe and Jean Gastiger, George Kalamaras, John Levy, Becky Parfitt, Susan and Christopher Porterfield. And especially and always to Jana.

Thanks, also, to the editors of the following publications where these poems appeared, often in earlier versions:
Anvil Tongue: "Be It So: You shadow me" and "Dear Morpheus, Though it's already"
Arsenic Lobster: "Dear Morpheus, Long ago"
Calibanonline: "Dear Morpheus, This Too Is Topographically True," "Dear Morpheus, Yes, I once," "Dear Morpheus, You lose your way," "Whereas: If you love"
Cider Press Review: "Whereas: 1962"
Gargoyle: "Whereas: *I must feed*"
Kerf: "Whereas: After we're gone"
Lake Effect: "Whereas, Holding the sculpture"
No Exit: "Whereas: Maybe I left it"
Pacific Poetry: "Whereas: That first time"
Pedestal: "Whereas: A moist anonymous"
Puerto del Sol: "Whereas: The man who repaired"
Rhino: "Dear Morpheus, Dad back home"
Sangham: "Be It So: I let slide" and "Dear Morpheus, I was gathering"
Spontaneous Mummification (SurVision Books, 2020): "Dear Morpheus, I breathe *allegro*" and "Dear Morpheus, I breathe Ten Sleep"
SurVision: "Dear Morpheus, Speak" and "Dear Morpheus, That shirt"

Terminus: "Be It So: There is only"
Waterwheel Review: "Be It So: The Nile, as seen"
Wild Gods: The Ecstatic in Contemporary American Poetry
      (New Rivers Press, 2021): "Dear Morpheus, I breathe
      allegro" and "Dear Morpheus, The smell"

ABOUT THE AUTHOR

JOHN BRADLEY was born in Brooklyn, New York, and grew up in Framingham, Massachusetts; Lincoln and Omaha, Nebraska; Massapequa and Lynbrook, New York; and Wayzata, Minnesota. His first book, *Love-in-Idleness: The Poetry of Robert Zingarello*, won the Washington Prize, in 1989, and a second edition, expanded and revised, was published by Work Works. Besides writing poetry, he is also fond of composing aphorisms, some of which appear in the anthologies *Short Flights* and *Short Circuits*. He's been a reviewer of poetry books for *Rain Taxi* for many years. The recipient of two National Endowment for the Arts Fellowships, a Pushcart Prize, and a grant from the Illinois Arts Council, he's currently a poetry editor for *Cider Press Review*. He lives in DeKalb, Illinois, with his wife, Jana, and their cats, Kiki and Zuzu.

www.ingramcontent.com/pod-product-compliance
Lightning Source LLC
Chambersburg PA
CBHW021653120626
46545CB00002B/839